The Ultimate

Baby Name

Book

By

Andrea Ludwig

Table of Contents

INTRODUCTION

So why is this book *The Ultimate*? Because it makes finding that perfect name simple, efficient, and fun! *The Ultimate Baby Name Book* is a compilation of the very best (in my humble opinion), most intriguing, interesting, and amazing baby names you will find. First is a list of 500 names for girls, with their origins and meanings. Then is a list of 500 names for boys, all alphabetically organized for your convenience. (The names with no origin or meaning listed are fictional/made-up.)

Lists with thousands of names to pour over are overwhelming and inefficient. This book was designed to provide you with an enjoyable time of finding your favorite names quickly and easily. In addition to the usual, familiar names, there is also a plethora of more unique names which may just inspire you to create a new baby name all your own.

Spark your imagination and begin reading. Enjoy!

But first, a few short and helpful tips:

INITIALS

When choosing a name for your baby, there are many things to consider – and one of them is initials. You don't want to be like the parents who were going to name their baby girl Allison Sophia Stevenson.

SOUND

Say the name you are considering out loud, the whole name – first, middle and last. Do you like the sound of it? Is it easy for you and others to pronounce?

SPELLING

Do you prefer a common spelling or an unusual one? If unusual, do you mind that people will, at times, misspell your child's name? Also, some spellings make the name hard for someone to decipher and pronounce. I'm thinking of teachers. Will a substitute teacher be able to pronounce the name when taking attendance?

I have a friend named Lyssa. It's pronounced just like "Lisa." But it sure looks like Lyssa ("Lissa") to me. Perhaps you don't mind if the pronunciation of the name is hard decipher from the spelling. It is rather fun for your child to have a very unique and mysterious name. At least your child's closest friends and your family will get it right.

ALLITERATION

Do you really want to put a bunch of Ls together? Lucy Lilliana Ludwig. That would be a mouthful. But maybe you like it…. It's up to you!

RUNNING TOGETHER

Consider the last letter (or sound) of the first name you have chosen, along with the first letter of your last name. You may not want them to be the same. For instance, you may want to stay away from names that end in the L sound, like Nicole or Chantal if your last name starts with L, because it will all run together. Also check the first name with the middle name for the same thing. Some examples are Marie Yvette and Hannah Amanda. You want to be writing poetry here, with the rhythm of your child's name.

SYLLABLES

Many people like to mix up the number of syllables in the first, middle, and last names. If your last name is two syllables, maybe you want your child's first name to be one or three or four syllables. Some people don't like the sound of a matching number of syllables. Consider, for example, the name Brett Wynn. What do you think? Or, consider Chloe Roberts. Not so bad. But you get the idea. Just consider the rhythm of the name and see if you like it.

NATIONALITY

You might want to make sure the nationality of the first name matches the last. For instance, Ian Kelly – both Irish names. It may sound strange if the first name is of a vastly different nationality from the last.

NICKNAMES

If you like a name, try to come up with a host of the nicknames that may go with it, to see if you like them. Even if you vow to call your child by only his or her full name, it's likely the kids at school will shorten it. Thinking of that, it's likely the kids will come up with some unappealing, offensive, and name-calling type name for your child if possible. So think like a bully when choosing your child's name and see if the name can be twisted and ruined. If it can, you might want to choose something less dangerous.

And now for the lists!

NAMES FOR GIRLS

Acacia – Hebrew – "thorny"

Ada –Old English – "prosperous"

Adalicia – French – "noble"

Adalyn – French – "of good humor"

Adara – Irish – "from the ford at the oak tree"

Addyson – English – "awesome"

Adela – French – "of good humor"

Adelia – French – "noble"

Adelina – French – "noble"

Adelle – French – "noble, kind"

Adelynn – French – "of good humor"

Adena – Hebrew – "sensuous"

Adreanna – French – "of the Adriatic Sea region"

Aenea – Hebrew – "worthy of praise"

Afton – Swedish – "afternoon"

Aidan – Irish – "fire"

Aileen – Irish – "light"

Ailisa – Irish – "noble"

Aimee – French – "beloved"

Airlia – Greek – "ethereal"

Aisley – English – "from the ash tree grove"

Aithne – Irish – "fire"

Alaine – Irish – "beautiful"

Alanna – Greek – "beautiful"

Alarise –German – "she rules all"

Alastrina – Irish – "avenger"

Albertyne – German – "noble"

Aldora – Greek – "winged gift"

Alecia – English – "beautiful queen"

Aleris – Greek – "from a city near the sea"

Alethea – Greek – "girl to be trusted"

Alexa – Greek – "helper, defender"

Alexandra – Greek – "helper of mankind"

Aleydis – Greek – "patient friend"

Alicia – Greek – "honest"

Alida – Greek – "from the city of fine clothes"

Alina – Irish – "beautiful"

Alissa – Greek – "pretty"

Allete – French – "winged"

Althea – Greek – "wholesome"

Alura – English – "divine counselor"

Alyanna – German – "vibrant"

Alysia – Greek – "of a possessive nature"

Alyssa – Greek – "rational"

Alyssandra – French – "defender"

Amalie – French – "striving"

Amara – Latin – "beloved"

Amaryllis – Greek – "fresh & new"

Amber – French – "the amber jewel"

Amberlee – English – "fossilized resin"

Ambrosine – Greek – "she is immortal"

Amelia – Latin – "industrious"

Amelie – French – "hard-working"

Amethyst – Greek – "precious stone"

Aminta – Greek – "protected"

Anastasia – Greek – "one who will rise again"

Anatola – Greek – "of the east"

Andrea – Italian – "womanly"

Andromeda – Greek – "the justice of the Lord"

Angela – Greek – "heavenly messenger"

Angelina – Greek – "God's messenger"

Annalise – German – "God's bountiful grace"

Anouk – French – "grace"

Anthea – Greek – "like a flower"

Antoinette – French – "beyond praise"

Apollonia – Greek – "strong"

April – English "the month of April"

Areta – Greek – "virtuous friend"

Aretina – Greek – "virtuous"

Ariadne – Greek – "holy one"

Ariana – Greek – "holy one"

Arielle – French – "lion of God"

Arietta – Italian – "melody"

Arina – Greek – "woman of peace"

Ashelynn – English – "meadow of ash trees"

Ashley – English – "from the ash tree grove"

Ashten – English – "from the town of ash trees"

Astrid – Scandinavian – "divine strength"

Athena – Greek – "wise"

Aubrey – French – "from the ash tree meadow"

Audreana – English – "nobility"

Aurelia – Latin – "golden"

Austina – Latin – "to increase"

Avalee – Latin – "bird"

Aveline – French – "nut"

Azura – French – "blue"

Bailey – English – "courtyard within castle walls"

Belle – French – "beautiful"

Bevin – Irish – "singer"

Bliss – English – "joy"

Braedyn – English – "broad hill"

Bree – Irish – "hill"

Breena – Irish – "fairy palace"

Brendolyn – Irish – "beacon on the hill"

Brenna – Celtic – "maiden with raven hair"

Brett – French – "from England"

Brezziana – English – "full of energy"

Briana – Irish – "strong"

Briashton

Brielle – Irish – "hill"

Brinlee

Brione – English – "flowering vine"

Brittany – English – "from England"

Brooke – English – "stream"

Bryn – Welsh – "hill"

Bryony – Greek – "flower"

Cacia – Irish – "vigilant"

Cailey – Greek – "lark"

Cailin – Irish – "girl"

Caitlin – Greek – "pure"

Calandra – Greek – "lark"

Calantha – Greek – "lovely blossom"

Callia – Greek – "beautiful voice"

Callista – Greek – "most lovely"

Cambria – Welsh – "country"

Caprice – Italian – "impulsive"

Cara – Celtic – "friend"

Carina – French – "pure"

Carissa – Greek – "gracious, kind"

Cassandra – Greek – "the prophetess"

Cassidy – Irish – "clever"

Catalina – Greek – "pure"

Catriona – Irish – "pure"

Cayleigh – Greek – "pure meadow"

Celene – Greek – "moon"

Chandra – Sanskrit – "she outshines the stars"

Chanel – French – "channel"

Chantae – French – "to sing"

Chantalle – French – "singer"

Charissa – Greek – "hope"

Charlotte – French – "little, womanly"

Charmaine – French – "song"

Chelsea – Old English – "seaport"

Cherisa – English – "dear one"

Cherise – French – "cherry"

Cheyenne – French – "of the Algonquian tribe"

Chiara – Irish – "dark"

Chloe – Greek – "fresh blooming"

Christa – Greek – "anointed"

Christabel – Latin – "follower of Christ"

Christiane – French – "follower of Christ"

Christina – Greek – "follower of Christ"

Cimberleigh

Cinderella – French – "little one among the ashes"

Cipriana – Greek – "from Cyprus"

Claire – French – "clear, bright"

Clara – French – "bright"

Clarissa – Latin – "shining"

Cleantha – English – "glory"

Clementina – French – "mercy"

Cleodel – Greek – "from a famous place"

Cleonie – Irish – "daughter"

Cleva – English – "dweller at the cliffs"

Clyte – Greek – "looking toward the sun"

Colene – Irish – "girl"

Colette – French – "necklace"

Cora – Greek – "maiden"

Coreen – Irish – "maiden"

Corina – Greek – "powerful"

Corinne – French – "maiden"

Corissa – English – "maiden"

Cosimia – Greek – "from the universe"

Courtlyn – French – "courteous"

Courtney – French – "from the court"

Cressida – Greek – "golden one"

Cristabel – French – "beautiful Christian"

Crystal – Greek – "sparkling"

Cynarra – Greek – "daughter of the moon"

Cyne – English – "ruler"

Danelle – Hebrew – "God will judge"

Dariela – French – "dear one"

Daryll – English – "dearly loved"

Davianna – English – "beloved"

Delphina – Greek – "dolphin"

Demetria – Greek – "of the harvest"

Desiree – French – "longed for"

Desma – Greek – "child of a vow"

Devony – Irish – "dark-haired"

Devyn – Gaelic – "servant"

Diantha – Greek – "flower"

Dianthe – Greek – "flower"

Dominique – French – "born on Sunday"

Dorinda – Greek – "bountiful gift"

Ebony – Greek – "strength"

Ecaterina – Greek – "innocent"

Echo – Greek – "echo"

Edelina – German – "gracious"

Eevee – English – "a Christmas Eve baby"

Eirene – Greek – "peace"

Elaina – French – "shining light"

Electra – Greek – "brilliant star"

Eleni – Greek – "light"

Elethea – Greek – "truth"

Eliane – French – "daughter of the sun"

Elisabet – Greek – "devoted to God"

Elise – French – "consecrated to God"

Elissa – "my God is bountiful"

Elita – French – "chosen"

Ella – French – "all"

Elle – French – "she"

Ellecia – Hebrew – "God is salvation"

Elodie – Greek – "fragile flower"

Elora – English – "God gives the crown of victory"

Elthia – Greek – "healer"

Emele – French – "admiring"

Emma – German – "whole, complete"

Erianthe – Greek – "sweet"

Eudora – Greek – "wonderful gift"

Eugenie – French – "well-born"

Eulalia – Greek – "a soft-spoken woman"

Euphemia – Greek – "fairest of the famous"

Evadne – Greek – "the little nymph"

Evangeline – Greek – "bearer of good news"

Evania – Greek – "child of peace"

Evanthe – Greek – "from a flower blossom"

Evelina –Hebrew – "life"

Everly – Old English – "boar meadow"

Evony – French – "archer"

Fabienne – French – "bean grower"

Fae – English – "faith"

Falon – Irish – "in charge"

Farrah – Middle English – "pleasant"

Farron – Irish – "adventurous"

Fawn – French – "young deer"

Fawna – English – "young deer"

Fay – French – "fairy"

Fayela – English – "faith and beauty"

Fierra

Finley – Irish – "fair-haired"

Fionna – Irish – "fair"

Flair – English – "style"

Fleur – French – "flower"

Gabriela – Hebrew – "God's capable one"

Gabrielle – French – "God is able"

Galatea – Greek – "ivory"

Galea – Hebrew – "fountain"

Gemma – French – "jewel"

Genaya – Celtic – "white wave"

Geneva – French – "juniper tree"

Genevieve – French – "white wave"

Gillian – Greek – "youthful"

Giselle – French – "pledge"

Greer – Greek – "the watchwoman"

Hadley –English – "field of heather"

Hailey – English – "field of hay"

Halley – Greek – "tranquil"

Haven – English – "heaven"

Hermione – Greek – "of the earth"

Hesper – Greek – "night star"

Hyacinthe – Greek – "purple"

Ianthe – Greek – "purple flower"

Idola – Greek – "lovely vision"

Ileana – Greek – "shining one"

Inesa – Greek – "innocent"

Iona – Greek – "purple jewel"

Iris – Greek – "rainbow"

Isabel – Hebrew – "my God is bountiful"

Isadora – Greek – "a gift"

Islene – Irish – "vision"

Iva – French – "from the yew tree"

Ivory – English – "white"

Ivy – Greek – "ivy"

Jacinda – Greek – "beautiful"

Jacinthe – French – "hyacinth"

Jacolin – Irish – "beauty"

Jacqueline – French – "supplanter"

Jade – English – the stone, jade

Jarina – Greek – "farmer"

Jasmyn – French – "flower"

Jeslyn – French – "blessed with wealth and beauty"

Jilliane – Latin – "love's child"

Jocelyn – French – "playful"

Joia – English – "rejoicing"

Joleigh – French – "pretty"

Jolie – French – "pretty"

Jordanna – Hebrew – "flowing down"

Julianna – Greek – "youthful"

Juliette – French – "youthful"

Justine – Latin – "upright"

Kaelah – Hebrew – "crowned with laurel"

Kaia – Hawaiian – "sea"

Kalista – Greek – "beautiful one"

Kambria – Spanish – "change"

Kamryn – Celtic – "crooked nose"

Kara – Italian – "beloved"

Kareena – Italian – "beloved"

Karina – Italian – "dear, beloved"

Karis – Greek – "grace and kindness"

Kasia – Greek – "pure"

Kassidy – Celtic – "curly-haired"

Katina – Greek – "pure"

Katrina – Greek –"pure"

Kayleigh – Irish – "slender"

Keanna – Irish – "ancient"

Kecia – Hebrew – "great joy"

Keeley – Irish – "lively"

Keira – Irish – "dark-haired"

Kelsey – Irish – "brave"

Kendra – Celtic – "greatest champion"

Kendyl – Old English – "the royal valley of Kent"

Kensleigh – English – "king's meadow"

Keva – Celtic – "beautiful child"

Kevay – Irish – "charming"

Khrystalline – English – "sparkling"

Kimbra – Old English – "from the royal fortress meadow"

Kira – Celtic – "dark"

Kirsten – Latin – "follower of Christ"

Koren – Greek – "pure"

Kresten – Latin – "Christian"

Kriesta

Krynn – Greek – "maiden"

Kyrie – Persian – "throne"

Lacey – Greek – "lovely"

Lainey – Hawaiian – "heaven"

Lais – Greek – "the adored"

Lalita – Sanskrit – "desirable"

Lana – Celtic – "harmony"

Larissa – Greek – "cheerful"

Lark – English – "lark"

Lashea – Celtic – "admirable"

Lauriel – Latin – "the laurel tree"

Leala – French – "faithful"

Leana – French – "vine"

Leandra – Greek – "like a lioness"

Leena – Irish – "wet meadow"

Lelia – French – "lily"

Levane – Irish – "elm tree"

Lexy – Greek – "defender of mankind"

Lianna – Greek – "daughter of the sun"

Liesl – Hebrew – "my God is bountiful"

Lindy – Italian – "beautiful"

Linette – French – "the linnet bird"

Luca – Latin – "light"

Lyndsey – Old English – "lake"

Lyssa – Greek – "lovely"

Maci – French – "weapon"

Mackinzie – Scottish – "son of Kenneth"

Madison – English – "child of Maude"

Maeve – Irish – "joy"

Maire – Irish – "bitter"

Malina – Hebrew – "from a high tower"

Mallory – French – "strong"

Mara – Hebrew – "bitter"

Marie – French – "bitter"

Marina – Latin – "sea maiden"

Marlaina – Hebrew – "woman from Magdala"

Mavis – French – "thrush"

Melania – Greek – "dark"

Melanie – Greek – "darkness"

Melantha – Greek – "dark flower"

Melina – Latin – "honey"

Meridel – Hebrew – "bitterness"

Merle – French – "blackbird"

Metea – Greek – "gentle"

Michaela – Hebrew – "gift from God"

Miranda – Latin –"to be admired"

Mireille – French – "to admire"

Moria – Hebrew – "bitterness"

Murel – Irish – "familiar with the sea"

Murielle – Hebrew – "bitter"

Myla – Slavonic – "merciful"

Nara – English – "nearest"

Narkissa – Greek – "sleep"

Nastassia – Greek – "resurrection"

Natalie – Latin – "child of Christmas"

Neely – Celtic – "champion"

Neoma – Hebrew – "sweetness"

Nerine – Greek – "nymph of the sea"

Nerissa – Greek – "of the sea"

Neysa – Greek – "pure"

Nicole – Greek – "victory of the people"

Nipha – Greek – "snowflake"

Noelle – French – "born on Christmas Day"

Obelia – Greek – "rich"

Octavia – Latin – "the eighth-born"

Odele – Greek – "a melody"

Odelia – German – "prosperous"

Odessa – Greek – "wrathful"

Olesia – "Greek – protector"

Olexa – Greek – "defender"

Ophelia – Greek – "wise"

Orea – Greek – "from the mountain"

Oriana – Celtic – "girl with white skin"

Orielle – Latin – "fair"

Orlaithe – Irish – "golden"

Orlena – Latin – "golden"

Paige – Old English – "young"

Pallas – Greek – "the wise maiden"

Pamela – Greek – "honeyed"

Parthenia – Greek – "chaste"

Pega – Greek – "joined together"

Penelope – Greek – "weaver"

Penthea – Greek – "fifth child"

Peony – English – "flower"

Perry – French – "pear tree"

Persis – Greek – "girl of peace"

Petra – Greek – "rock"

Petrina – Greek – "resolute"

Peyton – English –"town of the peacock"

Philana – Greek – "friend of mankind"

Philippa – Greek – "lover of horses"

Phillida – Greek – "loving woman"

Philomena – Greek – "loving friend"

Pier – French – "rock"

Piper – English – "piper"

Pippa – Greek – "lover of horses"

Psyche – Greek – "the soul"

Quintina – Latin – "the fifth child"

Rachel – Hebrew – "naïve and innocent"

Raegan – Irish – "spiritual strength"

Raphaela – Hebrew – "blessed healer"

Ravyn – English – "wise"

Remy – French – "from Rheims"

Rena – Hebrew – "joyous song"

Renee – French – "reborn"

Rhea – Greek – "motherly"

Riley – Irish – "island meadow"

Riona – Irish – "royal"

Riva – French – "shore"

Roanna – Latin – "sweet"

Rochelle – French – "from the little rock"

Rowan – Gaelic – "little red one"

Rowena – Celtic –"flowing white hair"

Ruby – French – "ruby"

Ruelle – French – "wolf"

Sabrina – Old English – "legendary princess"

Sacha – Greek – "helpmate"

Sage – English – "wise"

Salena – Latin – "salty"

Sapphira – Hebrew – jewel"

Scarlett – English – "red"

Seana – Irish – "present"

Selena – Greek – "moon"

Seraphina – Hebrew – "devout"

Shaelynn – Irish – "descendant of the fortunate one"

Shanaye – Irish – "beautiful one from a fairy palace"

Sinead – Irish – "God is gracious"

Sirena – Greek – "sweet singer"

Skyler – Dutch – "wise scholar"

Skylor – Irish – "eagle"

Sonia – Greek – "wisdom"

Sophia – Greek – "wisdom"

Starr – Old English – "star"

Stephanie – Greek – "crown"

Sydney – Hebrew – "the enticer"

Sylvia – Latin – "from the forest"

Tabitha – Aramaic – "gazelle"

Tallia – Hebrew – "dew from God"

Tara – Celtic – "tower"

Tassa – Russian – "born at Christmas"

Tatiana – Celtic –"silver-haired"

Tawnee – Irish – "a green field"

Teagan – Irish – "beautiful"

Teela – English –"blue-green"

Tessa – Greek – "harvest"

Thais – Greek – "giving joy"

Thalia – Greek – "blooming"

Thea – Greek – "God's divine gift"

Themis – Greek – "justice"

Theola – Greek – "heaven-sent"

Theone – Greek – "godly"

Thera – Greek – "untamed"

Thisbe – Greek – "the lost lover"

Thomasina – Hebrew – "the twin"

Tia – Latin – "joy"

Tiffany – Greek – "manifestation of God"

Tori – Latin – "triumphant"

Treise – Irish – "strong"

Tristina – Celtic – "sorrowful"

Tullia – Irish – "peaceful"

Tyler – English – "tile maker"

Tyna – English –"river"

Ulani – Hawaiian – "cheerful"

Una – Latin – "one"

Urania –Greek – "heavenly"

Valentina – Latin – "vigorous"

Vanessa – Greek – "butterfly"

Velvet – English – "soft"

Verity – Latin – "truth"

Veronica – Latin – "she brings victory"

Vevina – Irish – "sweet lady"

Vianca – Italian – "pure"

Victoria – Latin – "victorious"

Vivianna – Latin – "lively"

Wendelin – Anglo Saxon – "wanderer"

Whitley – English – "white meadow"

Wren – English – "wren"

Wynne – Celtic- "fair"

Xanthe – Greek – "blond"

Xena – Greek – "hospitable"

Xenia – Greek – "welcome"

Xylia – Greek – "of the wood"

Yvonne – French – "archer"

Zabrina – Old English – "of the nobility"

Zaira – Irish – "princess"

Zara – Hebrew – "the coming dawn"

Zena – Greek – "hospitable"

Zoe – Greek – "life"

Zora – Latin – "dawn"

Zosima – Greek – "full of life"

NAMES FOR BOYS

Aaric – Scandinavian – "kingly, rules with mercy"

Aaron – Hebrew – "exalted"

Abbott – Arabic – "father"

Abel – Hebrew –"breath"

Ace – Latin – "unity"

Achilles – Greek – "swift"

Ackley – Old English – "from the oak meadow"

Adair – Scottish – "from the oak tree ford"

Adam – Hebrew – "man of the red earth"

Addison – Old English –"son of Adam"

Adin – Hebrew – "attractive"

Adlai – Hebrew – "my witness"

Adler – German – "eagle"

Adonis – Greek – "handsome"

Adriel – Hebrew – "of God's flock"

Adrien – Latin –"dark"

Aeneas – Greek – "worthy of praise"

Aiden –Gaelic – "little fire"

Aiken – Old English – "the oaken"

Ainsley – English – "meadow"

Ajax – Greek – "eagle"

Alaric – German – "noble ruler"

Alden – Old English – "old friend"

Alec – Greek – "defender"

Aleron – Latin – "the winged"

Alex – Greek – "defender of mankind"

Alexander – Greek – "protector"

Alger – German – "noble spearman"

Alistair – Scottish – "helper of mankind"

Amery – German – "divine rule"

Amias – Latin – "loved"

Amsden

Anastatius – Italian – "one who is reborn"

Anatole – Greek – "of the east"

Ander – Swedish – "manly"

Anderson – Swedish – "son of Andee"

Andre – French – "manly"

Andrew – Greek – "manly"

Andric – Greek – "manly"

Angell – Italian – "angel"

Angelo – Italian – "angel"

Anlon – Irish – "champion"

Ansel – French – "God's protection"

Ansley – Old English – "from the meadow"

Anson – Old English – "son of a noble"

Anstice – Middle English – "resurrected"

Antoine – French – "praiseworthy"

Apollo – Greek – "beautiful man"

Aralt – Irish – "leader"

Arden – Latin – "ardent"

Ardley – English – "from the home-lover's meadow"

Aries – Latin – "a ram"

Arland – Hebrew – "pledge"

Armand – German – "soldier"

Armstrong – English – "strong-armed"

Aron – Hebrew – "inspired"

Asher – Hebrew – "happy"

Ashley – Old English – "from the ash tree meadow"

Ashton – English – "from the ash tree farm"

Assan – Irish – "waterfall"

Aubrey – French – "elf ruler"

Augustin – French – "majestic"

Augustine – Latin – "majestic, exalted"

Austin – Latin – "exalted"

Avery – French – "elf ruler"

Azaiah – Hebrew – "God is my strength"

Azriel – Hebrew – "eagle of the Lord"

Bailey – Latin – "steward"

Baird – Irish – "ballad singer"

Bane – Hawaiian – "long-awaited child"

Banning – Irish – "little blond one"

Barclay – Old English – "from the birch tree meadow"

Barlow – English – "lives on the bare hill"

Baron – Old English – "nobleman"

Barric – English – "grain farm"

Bartleigh – English – "from Bart's meadow"

Basile – French – "kingly"

Baxter – Old English – "baker"

Bay – Latin – "berry"

Beau – French – "handsome"

Beck – German – "brook"

Bellamy – French – "beautiful friend"

Benen – Irish – "blessed"

Benjamin – Hebrew – "born of the right hand"

Benson – English – "son of Benedict"

Benton – Old English – "from the winding meadow"

Beore – English – "birch tree"

Berke – English – "from the birch tree meadow"

Berkeley – Old English – "birch meadow"

Bevan – Irish – "young archer"

Blade – English – "wealthy glory"

Blaine – Irish – "thin"

Blair – Irish – "from the fields"

Blaise – French – "stammerer"

Blake – Old English – "light-complected and fair-haired"

Blakely – English – "from the dark meadow"

Bogart – Danish – "strong as a bow"

Bond – Old English – "tiller of the soil"

Boone – French – "good"

Boyce – French – "from the woodland"

Braden – Old English – "broad hillside"

Brady – Old English – "from the broad island"

Brandon – Old English – "from the beacon hill"

Brant – Old English – "proud"

Brendan – Irish – "sword"

Brent – Old English – "from the high hill"

Brett – Celtic – "native of Brittany"

Brice – Welch – "valor"

Brick – Yiddish – "bridge"

Brock – Old English – "a badger"

Broderick – Old English – "from the broad ridge"

Bronson – Old English – "son of the brown one"

Brooks – Old English – "he dwells by the stream"

Bruce – French – "from the brush"

Burgess – Old English – "citizen of a fortified town"

Burke – French – "fortress dweller"

Byron – English – "from the cottage"

Cace – Irish – "vigorous"

Cade – Welsh – "spirit of the battle"

Caesar – Latin – "long-haired"

Caine – Hebrew – "gatherer"

Calder – Old English – "stream"

Caleb – Hebrew – "bold"

Calix – Latin – "chalice"

Calloway – Irish – "rocky place"

Camden – Scottish – "the winding valley"

Cameron – Scottish – "crooked nose"

Carew – Celtic – "from this fortress"

Carson – Welsh – "son of the marsh dweller"

Carter – Old English – "maker of carts"

Cavan – Irish – "hollow"

Chad – Celtic – "defender"

Chamberlain – Old English – "keeper of the house"

Chance – English – "fortune"

Chandler – French – "candle maker"

Chane – French – "dependable"

Channing – English – "young wolf"

Chase – French – "hunter"

Chaunce – English – "chancellor"

Chayne – French – "oak"

Christian – Greek – "follower of Christ"

Christopher – Greek – "Christ-bearer"

Clark – French – "a learned man, scholar"

Clayton – Old English – "from the clay town"

Cluny – Gaelic – "from the meadow"

Cole – Latin – "the dove"

Colin – Irish – "strong"

Connor – Celtic – "wise"

Crispin – Latin – "curly-haired"

Cullen – Irish – "handsome"

Curtis – French – "courteous"

Cuyler – Gaelic – "devoted"

Cyprian – Latin – "man of Cyprus"

Daire – Irish – "wealthy"

Dallas – Scottish – "skilled"

Dalton – Old English – "from the farm in the dell"

Damon – Greek – "tame"

Daric – Gaelic – "strong-hearted"

Darien – Greek – "gift"

Darius – Greek – "wealthy"

Darrel – French – "beloved"

Davin – Scandinavian – "the bright man"

Dayne – English – "from Denmark"

Delmore – French – "from the sea"

Demetrius – Greek – "lover of the earth"

Derek – German – "ruler"

Deron – Gaelic – "great"

Devin – Irish – "poet"

Dillon – Irish – "faithful"

Dirk – German –"ruler of the people"

Dominic – Latin – "belonging to the Lord"

Donnelly – Irish – "brave dark man"

Donovan – Irish – "brown-haired warrior"

Doran –Celtic – "a stranger"

Dorian – Greek – "from the sea"

Drake – Middle English – "swan"

Drew – French – "skilled, honest"

Duke – Latin – "leader"

Duncan – Scottish – "dark-skinned warrior"

Dustin – German – "strong-hearted leader"

Dylan – Welsh –"son of the wave"

Eagan – Irish – "fiery"

Eamon – Irish – "guardian of the riches"

Eli – Hebrew – "ascended"

Elias – Greek – "Jehovah is God"

Elijah – Hebrew –"Jehovah is God"

Ellery – Old English – "from the elder tree island"

Elliot – Hebrew – "Jehovah is God"

Ellis – Hebrew – "Jehovah is God"

Emerson – German – "son of the industrious ruler"

Emery – German – "industrious ruler"

Endre – Greek – "manly"

Eneas – Irish – "praise"

Erasmus – Greek – "kind"

Erastus – Greek – "honored son"

Eric – Scandinavian – "kingly"

Espen – Dutch – "bear"

Ethan – Hebrew – "firm"

Etienne – French – "crown"

Eugene – Greek – "noble"

Evan – Welsh –"a youth"

Evander – Scottish – "well-doer"

Everett – Old English – "strong as a boar"

Everhart – Dutch – "brave boar"

Ezekiel – Hebrew – "strength of God"

Fabian – Latin – "bean grower"

Farrell – Irish – "valiant"

Favian – Latin – "a man of understanding"

Faxon – German – "renowned for his hair"

Finn – Irish – "white, fair"

Fisk – Scandinavian – "the fisherman"

Forbes –Irish – "prosperous"

Forrest – French – "of the forest"

Frazer – French – "strawberry"

Fremont – German –"guardian of freedom"

Gabriel – Hebrew – "man of God"

Gage – French – "pledge, promise"

Gaige – English – "measurer"

Galvin – Celtic – "sparrow"

Garen – German – "guardian"

Gareth – Welsh –"gentle"

Garner – French – "armed sentry"

Garrett – Old English – "skilled with the spear"

Garrick – Old English – "spear-king"

Garson – Old English – "warrior"

Garth – Old Norse – "groundskeeper"

Gaston – French – "from Gascony"

Gavin – Welsh – "white hawk"

Geoffrey – French – "divine peace"

Gilles – Greek –"shield-bearer"

Glade – Old English – "sunny"

Grady – Irish – "noble"

Grant – Middle English – "great"

Grayson – Old English – "a judge's son"

Gregor – Dutch – "vigilant"

Gregory – Greek – "vigilant"

Greston

Griffith – Welsh – "strong Lord"

Gunther – Nordic – "warrior"

Gurias – Hebrew – "from a wandering family"

Guy – French – "guide"

Hadley – Old English – "from the heath meadow"

Hamilton – Old English – "from the mountain town"

Hamlin – French – "little home-lover"

Harlan – Old English – "army land"

Harlow – Old English – "from the fortified hill"

Harmon – Greek – "unifying"

Harper – Old English – "harp player"

Harris – Old English – "son of Henry"

Harrison – Old English –"son of Henry"

Hartley – Old English – "from the deer meadow"

Hayden – Old English – "from the hedge valley"

Heath – Middle English – "from the heath"

Henri – French – "ruler of his household"

Hewett – "little intelligent one"

Hilton – Old English –"the hill estate"

Hogan – Irish – "youth"

Houston – Old English – "hill town"

Hudson – Old English – "son of Hyde"

Hunter – Old English – "hunter"

Huntington – Old English – "hunting estate"

Huxley – Old English – "Hugh's meadow"

Isaiah – Hebrew – "salvation of the Lord"

Ivan – Russian –"glorious gift"

Ives – French – "archer"

Jace – Greek – "healing"

Jackson – Old English – "son of Jack"

Jacob – Hebrew – "supplanter"

Jaeden

Jago – Greek – "king"

Jair – Hebrew – "one whom God has enlightened"

Jake – Hebrew – "supplanter"

James – Hebrew – "supplanter"

Jameson – English – "supplanter"

Janson – Dutch – "son of Jan"

Jared – Hebrew – "descending"

Jaren – Hebrew – "descending"

Jarvis – Celtic – "servant's spear"

Jason – Greek – "healer"

Jax – English – "God has been gracious"

Jay – Old English – "blue jay"

Jayden – Hebrew – "Jehovah has heard"

Jed – Hebrew – "loved by the Lord"

Jedediah – Hebrew – "loved by the Lord"

Jeffrey – German – "peace"

Jerron – Hebrew – "to sing, shout"

Jett – Hebrew – "abundance"

Joaquim – Hebrew – "the Lord will judge"

Joel – Hebrew – "Jehovah is the Lord"

Jonah – Hebrew – "dove"

Jonathan – Hebrew – "Jehovah given"

Jordan – Hebrew – "from the river"

Jorian – Greek – "farmer"

Joshua – Hebrew – "Jehovah saves"

Josiah – Hebrew – "he is healed by the Lord"

Judd – Hebrew – "beloved descendant"

Jude – Hebrew – "praise"

Judson – German – "son of Judd"

Julian – Latin – "belonging to Julius"

Justin – Latin – "judicious"

Justus – Latin – "just, right, fair"

Kade – Scottish – "from the wetlands"

Kaeden – Arabic – "friend"

Kai – Hawaiian – "ocean"

Kalen – Gaelic – "warrior"

Kane – Celtic – "fighter"

Karsten – German – "blessed one"

Kavan – Irish – "handsome"

Keagan – Irish – "thinker"

Keanan – Irish –"ancient"

Kearn – Irish – "dark"

Keaton – English – "place of the hawks"

Keith – Scottish – "enclosed place"

Kelvin – English – "river man"

Kendrick – Irish – "son of Henry"

Kenley – English – "from the king's meadow"

Kennedy – Irish – "helmeted"

Kent – Welsh – "radiant"

Kevin – Irish –"gentle"

Kieran – Irish – "little and dark-skinned"

Kingsley – Old English – "from the king's meadow"

Kingston – Old English – "from the king's estate"

Knute – Norse – "knot"

Lach – English – "lives near water"

Laird – Scottish – "lord of the land"

Lance – Old English – "spear"

Landers – Greek – "lion"

Landon – Old English – "from the long hill"

Lane – Old English – "from the country road"

Langdon – English – "ridge"

Langley – Old English – "from the long meadow"

Langston – English – "from the tall man's estate"

Leander – Greek – "brave like a lion"

Lear – German – "joyful"

Leland – Old English – "of the meadowlands"

Leo – Latin – "lion"

Levi –Hebrew – "joined in harmony"

Lewis – German – "famous warrior"

Liam – Gaelic – "strong-willed warrior"

Logan – Scottish – "hollow meadow"

Luc – French – "illumination"

Lucien – French – "light"

Ludovic – Scottish – "famous warrior"

Luke – Latin – "light"

Lunden – English – "from London"

Lyle – French – "of the island"

Lysander – Greek – "liberator"

Marc – Latin – "a warrior"

Marlon – French – "little falcon"

Marshall – French – "caretaker of horses"

Mason – Latin – "stone worker"

Matthew – Hebrew – "God's gift"

Merle – French – "blackbird"

Meyer – German – "overseer"

Micah – Hebrew – "Like unto the Lord"

Michael – Hebrew – "God-like"

Montague – French – "from the pointed mountain"

Montgomery – French – "from the mountain castle"

Moore – Middle English – "marsh, open land"

Morrissey – Irish – "choice of the sea"

Nathan – Hebrew – "given by God"

Nathaniel – Hebrew – "gift of God"

Nevan – Irish – "holy"

Neville – French – "from the new town"

Nicholas – Greek – "victory of the people"

Nico – English – "victory"

Nicodemus – Greek – "victory of the people"

Nicolas – Greek – "conqueror"

Noah – Hebrew – "comfort, rest, peace"

Noel – French – "born at Christmas"

Nolan – Irish – "noble"

Norris – English – "from the north"

Nyke – Greek – "victory"

Oakley – Old English – "from the oak tree meadow"

Oran – Gaelic – "pale green"

Oren – Hebrew – "pine tree"

Orion – Latin – "giant"

Owen – Celtic – "young warrior"

Palmer – Latin – "the palm-bearer"

Parker – Middle English – "park keeper"

Pasquale – French – "born on Easter"

Patrick – Latin – "noble"

Paxton – Old English – "peaceful town"

Payton – Old English – "the fighter's estate"

Pearson – Irish – "rock"

Percy – English – "from Percy"

Perry – Old English – "pear tree"

Peter – Latin – "rock"

Peyton – Old English – "noble"

Philemon – Greek –"man of exceptional good looks"

Philip – Greek – "lover of horses"

Pierce – English – "rock"

Pierson – English – "son of Peter"

Pirro – Greek – "red-haired"

Plaise – Irish – "strong"

Quentin – Latin – "fifth"

Quincy – Latin – "the fifth son's estate"

Quinlan – Irish – "strong"

Quinn – Celtic – "high and mighty"

Radley – Old English – "from the red lea"

Rainger – French – "ward of the forest"

Ranen – Hebrew – "joyful song"

Ranier – French – "strong counselor"

Raphael – Hebrew – "healed by God"

Ray – Latin – "kingly"

Reade – Old English – "red-haired"

Reece – Welsh – "fiery one"

Reeve – Old English – "steward"

Regan – Irish – "little king"

Remi – English – "from the raven farm"

Reule – Hebrew – "friend of God"

Rian – Celtic – "kingly"

Ripley – Old English – "from the shouting man's meadow"

Roane – Celtic – "red-haired"

Roarke – Irish – "famous"

Roman – Latin – "from Rome"

Romney – Old English – "from the town of Romney

Roosevelt – Dutch – "from the field of roses"

Roque – Latin – "valiant soldier"

Rory – Celtic – "red king"

Ross – Scottish – "red"

Roy – French – "king"

Royce – Old English – "son of the king"

Russell – French – "red-haired"

Ryan – Irish – "little king"

Sage – English – "wise one"

Saire – German – "hermit"

Sanders – Greek – "son of Alexander"

Sargent – English – "officer"

Sawyer – Middle English – "wood saver"

Saxon – Old English – "sword people"

Sean – Hebrew – "gift from God"

Sebastian – Latin – "respected, revered"

Seth – Hebrew – "chosen"

Severin – Old English – "of the Severn River"

Sevrin – Latin – "strict, restrained"

Shane – Hebrew – "Jehovah has been gracious"

Sidney – French – "from St. Denis"

Sinclair – French – "from St. Clair"

Sloan – Celtic – "warrior"

Spencer – French – "storekeeper"

Sprague – Middle English – "lively"

Squire – English – "shield-bearer"

Stanford – Old English – "from the rocky ford"

Stephen – Greek – "crowned one"

Sterling – English – "standard of excellence"

Sullivan – Irish – "dark eyes"

Taber – Irish – "well"

Tad – Latin – "praising God"

Tait – Scandinavian – "of great joy"

Talon – French – "sharp"

Taryn – Welsh –"thunder"

Tavis – Scottish –"twin"

Terrence – Latin – "polished"

Tevin – Scottish – "twin"

Thane – Old English – "attendant"

Thanos – Greek – noble"

Thayer – Teutonic – "from the nation's army"

Theron – Greek – "hunter"

Timothy – Greek – "God-fearing"

Titus – Roman – "honor"

Todd – Scottish – "the fox"

Tor –Norse – "from the craggy hills"

Traigh – Irish – "strand"

Travis – English – "from the crossroads"

Trent – Latin – "swift"

Trevor – Celtic – "prudent"

Tristan – Latin – "sorrowful"

Troy – French – "curly-haired"

Turner – Middle English – "lathe worker"

Tyce – English – "fiery"

Tyler – Old English – " a tile maker"

Tyson – Teutonic – "son of a German"

Ulysses – Greek – "vengeful"

Uriah – Hebrew – "the Lord is my light"

Van – Dutch – "of"

Vance –Dutch –"son of Vandyke"

Vayle – French – "from the green hill"

Vromme – Dutch – "wise"

Wade – Old English – "one who moves forward"

Ward –Old English – "watchman"

Wesley – Old English – "from the west meadow"

Weston – Old English – "from the west town"

Wyatt – French – "little warrior"

Xanthus – Latin – "golden-haired"

Xavier – Arabic – "splendid"

Xenos – Greek – "the stranger"

Xerxes – Persian – "king"

Xylon – Greek – "of the forest"

Yale – Old English – "dweller from the side of the hill"

Yardley – Old English – "from the enclosed meadow"

Yates – Old English – "from the gates"

Yves – French – "archer"

Zachariah – Hebrew – "the Lord's remembrance"

Zale – Greek – "power of the sea"

Zane – Hebrew – "God's gracious gift"

Zarek – "God protect the king"

Zedekiah – Hebrew – "God is just"

Zeke – Hebrew – "God strengthens"

Zenon – Greek – "friendly"

Top 40 Most Popular Names in the U.S. in 2015

GIRLS – Listed alphabetically

- Abigail
- Amelia
- Aria
- Aubrey
- Audrey
- Ava
- Avery
- Brooklyn
- Claire
- Charlotte
- Chloe
- Ella
- Ellie
- Elizabeth
- Emma
- Emily
- Evelyn
- Grace
- Hannah
- Harper
- Isabella
- Layla
- Lillian
- Lily
- Lucy
- Madison

- Mia
- Mila
- Natalie
- Nora
- Olivia
- Penelope
- Riley
- Scarlett
- Sofia
- Sophia
- Victoria
- Zoe
- Zoey

BOYS – Listed alphabetically

- Aiden
- Alexander
- Andrew
- Benjamin
- Caleb
- Carter
- Connor
- Daniel
- David
- Dylan
- Eli
- Elijah
- Ethan
- Gabriel
- Grayson

- Henry
- Isaac
- Jack
- Jackson
- Jacob
- James
- Jaxon
- Jayden
- Joshua
- Liam
- Logan
- Lucas
- Luke
- Mason
- Matthew
- Michael
- Nathan
- Noah
- Oliver
- Owen
- Ryan
- Samuel
- Sebastian
- William
- Wyatt

Printed in Great Britain
by Amazon

52795777R00033